Believing is Seeing:
Why Spiritual Faith is Good for People

Timothy J. Houghton, Ph.D.

Stemmer Publishing
Rochester, Michigan

© Copyright 2010
Timothy J. Houghton, Ph.D.

All rights reserved. No part of this book may be reproduced in any form, except for the inclusion of brief quotations in a review, without permission in writing from the author or publisher.

ISBN: 978-1-935356-07-3

Please order at Amazon.com or contact
stemmerpublishing@houghtonandhoughton.com
for volume discounts

CATALOGING-IN-PUBLICATION DATA

Houghton, Timothy J., 1961-
　　Believing is seeing : why spiritual faith is good for people / Timothy J. Houghton.
　　p. cm.
　　Includes bibliographical references.
　　ISBN-13: 978-1-935356-07-3
　　ISBN-10: 1-935356-07-0

　　1. Faith. 2. Faith--Moral and ethical aspects.
　　3. Faith--Psychological aspects.　I. Title.

BV4637.H68 2010　　　　　　234'.23
　　　　　　　　　　　　　QBI10-600043

Manufactured in the United States of America

Table of Contents

Preface	v
Introduction	1
Religion	1
Sacred Writings	6
Common Ground	8
All or Nothing	9
Faith Helps People View Negative Happenings Positively	11
Faith Improves Attitude	15
Faith Teaches Patience	17
Faith Fosters Hope	19
Faith Cultivates Compassion	21
Faith Encourages Persistence	25
Faith Brings About Inner Peace	27
Faith Promotes Forgiving	31
Faith Encourages Mutual Respect	35
Faith Inspires People	39
Faith Helps Resolve Conflict	43
Faith Promotes Tolerance of Other Religions	47
Faith-Based Organizations (FBO)	53
Final Thoughts	59
References Cited	60

Preface

Many people confuse the terms *faith* and *religion*. They mistakenly think that the two words are synonymous, and often use them interchangeably. But an examination of the dictionary definitions of these two words shows that they are actually quite different.

The *American Heritage Dictionary* (1982) defines faith as:
- A confident belief in the truth, value or trustworthiness of a person, idea or thing.
- Belief that does not rest on logical proof or material evidence.
- Loyalty to a person or thing: allegiance.
- Belief and trust in God.
- A system of religious beliefs.
- A set of principles or beliefs.

This same dictionary defines religion as:
- Belief in and reverence for a supernatural power recognized as the creator and governor of the universe.
- A particular integrated system of the above expression.
- The spiritual or emotional attitude of one who recognizes the existence of a superhuman power or powers.
- An objective pursued with zeal or conscientious devotion.

A careful study of these definitions reveals that people can have faith without religion, they can have religion without faith, and they can have faith and religion combined. This book examines various faiths and religions that mankind pursues in its never-ending quest for inner peace.

This book was written to show the good that faith can bring about in this world. It was written using the support of facts, figures, quotations, and beliefs from a variety of faith-based writings, organizations, and people. It was written without condemning or condoning the specific doctrines followed by members of religions, sects, or other faith-based belief systems. It was written with the hope that it would inspire people to keep believing, or begin believing, in a spiritual power that guides them through life.

Introduction

What exactly is spiritual faith? Does it need to involve religion? Does it need to be based on sacred writings believed to be from a higher power? Does it need to find common ground among everyone? Does it need to be all or nothing? These thought provoking questions are often best answered by people using their individual feelings, beliefs, situations, and needs.

Religion

Many people believe that faith directly involves religion. This may be true, but religion poses many unanswered questions because it is an anomaly and a dichotomy. It enables people to reach a level of hope that is otherwise unattainable, yet scandals within can lead to a feeling of hopelessness. It makes complete sense to millions of worshipers, yet it can lead them to commit senseless acts. Some people have saved others based on their religious views, while others have killed for what is arguably the same God. Religion keeps people quiet and in line, but it also causes violent acts of expression. Religion brings people together and it also tears them apart, but it has been an important part of the human existence for thousands of years…enduring countless obstacles and opponents in the process.

Religion has long been associated with power, and sometimes that power is abused. Certain religious leaders might have initially set out with the intent of doing good things for people, and ultimately ended up doing bad things due to the position and power they usurped over time. Other leaders had bad intentions from the start and used religion to turn those intentions into reality. This book makes no attempt to defend these people or their actions, since they used their religious beliefs wrongly for personal gain. The premise of this writing promotes the positive aspects of spiritual faith, not specific religions or cults that utilize blind faith as a method of brainwashing their members.

Please note that established religions and their denominations, types, forms, and/or divisions are discussed at many points in this book. These discussions are formulated for example purposes to support the thinking that all faith is good. The intent is not to support, condone, or condemn any of the religions mentioned.

Also note that some people challenge the validity of religious beliefs. They question the idea of believing in something that has no material proof of existence. How can people believe in something they cannot see? The answer, of course, is faith. The difference between a person of faith and an atheist is that one can visualize the invisible and the other cannot.

The Council for Secular Humanism argues that the good stemming from deep religious faith is overestimated and misunderstood. In an article from their website, Phil Zuckerman (2008) talks about the misconceptions involving nations of little or no faith. He indicates that people might assume these nations are riddled with social problems, but in reality they actually have more law-abiding citizens, less sickness, and lower levels of poverty than those with strong religious foundations:

> The most secular countries – those with the highest proportion of atheists and agnostics – are among the most stable, peaceful, free, wealthy, and healthy societies. And the most religious nations – wherein worship of God is in abundance – are among the most unstable, violent, oppressive, poor, and destitute.

This is powerful and interesting research that many people of faith might find disturbing and puzzling. How could such a thing happen when faith helps people in difficult situations and guides them through life's journey? The answer comes from Zuckerman (2008), who continues with the following statement:

> Belief in God may provide comfort to the individual believer, but, at the societal level, its results do not compare at all favorably with that of the more secular societies.

The key here is "provides comfort to the individual believer." This book is not making an argument that zealous religion is the complete solution to all of the world's problems; it simply attempts to explain why spiritual faith, regardless of the encompassing negative happenings, is essentially good for people living in this world. No attempt is made to explain, defend, or attack specific beliefs, religions, or denominations; the goal is to merely show through example how basic faith betters individuals' lives. People from all nations progress through life asking questions…and faith provides some comforting answers.

Interestingly enough, research has found that more than nine in ten Americans have faith in God or some type of universal spirit (Smith, 2008). While not all of these people are absolutely certain that God exists, they do achieve common ground by having some degree of faith.

That common ground, however, does not mean that all people react similarly in response to their faith. Prayer exemplifies this quite well. Some people pray only at church because that is when they feel it is the proper time. Others attend church, but pray outside the physical boundaries, preferring a less public setting. Then there are those who pray and do not even attend church. In this case, their spiritual needs are not met by a congregation like they are by private prayer.

People also pray for different reasons. Some people pray because they want something. They might want to meet a special person with whom they can share the rest of their lives. Some pray because they need something. They might need a miracle in order to survive some type of illness. Still others pray because they are thankful for what they have. They may feel they have been blessed based on their experiences.

Most Americans pray in some form at some time, including those who are not affiliated with any religious organization. This is encouraging to spiritual believers, but it is also worthy of note that people belonging to specific religious denominations differ when it comes to frequency of prayer or meditation. Smith (2008) notes the following:

> Three-quarters of Americans report praying once a week, with large majorities among most religious traditions saying they pray at least this often. Even among the unaffiliated, people who are not associated with any particular religious tradition, roughly one in three pray on at least a weekly basis. At the same time, however, there are those among all faith groups who pray much less frequently. Overall, one-quarter of the public says they pray a few times a month or less often. In addition, almost two-fifths of Americans report meditating at least once a week. This practice is particularly common among Buddhists, with six in 10 saying they meditate weekly. But it's also interesting that nearly three-quarters of Jehovah's Witnesses, more than half of Mormons and members of historically black Protestant denominations, and nearly one-half of evangelical Protestants and Muslims say they meditate weekly. One-quarter of the unaffiliated population also reports meditating at least on a weekly basis.

Smith (2008) goes on to say that about one-third of Americans claim to receive specific answers to their prayers at least once a month. This indicates the power and importance of faith in these people's lives. The *ask and you shall receive* thinking is alive and well within the spiritual community.

Smith's (2008) research has some interesting findings on atheism. This is a complicated subject because some people who identify themselves as atheists are not necessarily stating that they do not believe in God or have faith. They are sometimes merely saying that they do not approve of any type of organized religion and that is why they have an association with atheism. This comment is understandable based on the abuse of religion that has occurred over the centuries.

Despite the negatives associated with certain organized religion, faith maintains an obvious appeal for millions of people. One only needs to look at Billy Graham to support this claim. For six decades, Graham led a crusade-based ministry that evolved around the world. He filled stadiums with believers wanting to hear his message, and he has counseled every United States president since Harry S. Truman. Just meeting that many presidents is a feat in itself…but getting them to listen to faith-based advice speaks mountains for believers in a higher power.

Understanding people's religious affiliations is often perplexing, but it can be explained by The Cyclical Theory of Religion and Perception (see Exhibit 1). This theory proposes that people analyze moral, ethical, social, and spiritual issues and develop religious beliefs in order to establish perception of themselves. Through common bond, they associate with individuals of the same religious viewpoints and disassociate with those who differ. This association and disassociation helps them establish a perception of how they see themselves and would like to be viewed by others. This perception is reinforced when they analyze other issues in life and make similar decisions based on their religious beliefs.

Issue → Religious Beliefs → Association with Similar → Establish Perception

Disassociation with Different

← Reinforce Perception ←

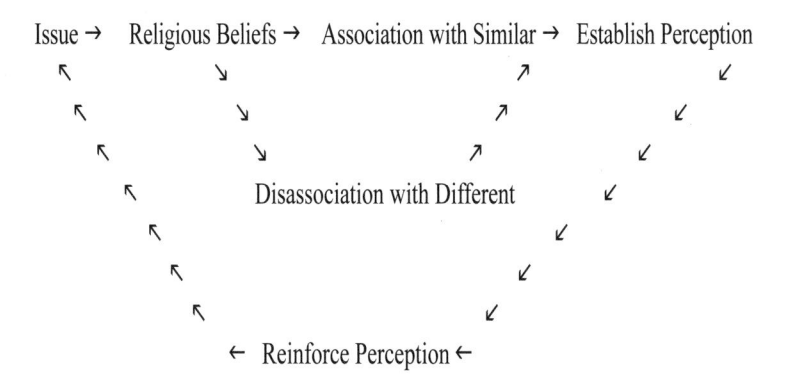

Exhibit 1: The Cyclical Theory of Religion and Perception

Sacred Writings

People like to see things in writing. The written word is preferred over verbal agreements for things such as buying a car, getting approval for a home mortgage, and setting a deadline for completion of a project. This is done for psychological and legal reasons, and it also establishes a sense of security because there is a track record of what transpired.

This thinking also applies to sacred writings. Sacred writings have been utilized by people as spiritual guidance for centuries. Some people tend to lean verbatim on the wording, while others translate it more loosely. Whatever the case, sacred writings serve some type of purpose for those who read them. That purpose, however, differs among the various faiths of the world. Lee Warren (n.d.) notes the following:

> Some groups believe that their holy books are direct pronouncements from God given to a particular prophet to begin a religion. Muslims claim that Allah revealed the Koran to Mohammed for just that purpose. Other sacred writings downplay the importance of written expression and stress that experience is superior to words. Buddhists believe that words are only signposts or maps pointing to the truth. Although the Buddha's teachings are written in the Pali Canons and Tripitakas, the entire Buddhist experience, especially Zen, centers on breaking the language barrier and not substituting words for the reality – an enlightened consciousness.

Despite the widespread use of faith-based documents, a question still arises. Does faith need to be based on writings of religious works such as the Bible, Qur'an, or Upanishads? This question will likely have a different answer depending on who is asked, and all opinions will most certainly not be the same. While books of divine guidance provide a religious framework for some, others do not understand them, nor do they possess the desire to do so. Faith can come from a combination of beliefs from sacred works, or from within oneself…without the help of any written rules or guidelines.

The interpretation of religious works also varies. People reading the same segment of writing might have different perceptions of exactly what that writing means and how it should be applied. Who is right and who is wrong? This is left purely to judgment based on personal experiences, which means there is no absolutely correct point of view. For example, many Christian denominations use the same Bible as a guiding resource. While beliefs are sometimes similar, they are not identical in all instances...just attend a Baptist, Lutheran, and Catholic service, and some of these similarities and differences will manifest themselves. Quite simply, interpretation of and inspiration from religious works often depends on the people reading them.

Other support for interpretative meaning points to the warring in Ireland between Protestants and Catholics. Religious disagreements have allowed this conflict to exist for years, yet they follow the same basic religious dogma.

Perception, interpretation, and opinion all play roles in understanding sacred writings. Because of this, it is difficult, if not impossible, to base faith on religious works alone. However, it can be noted that sacred writings are some of the most thought-suggesting and thought-provoking documents ever written.

Common Ground

Should all people of spiritual faith follow a similar path? Do they need to agree on everything when it comes to believing in a higher spiritual source? If the answer is *yes*, then that common ground needs to be defined; and it would be difficult, if not impossible, to find someone who could define it. Without that definition, the answer must be *no*.

An analogy to support *no* for an answer involves an essential function of life…eating. People need to eat in order to stay alive, but everyone does not eat the same food. Some will not eat vegetables, while others refuse to eat anything derived from animals. However, both types can live healthy lives if they consume the proper nutrition from the foods they choose to eat. This analogy can be loosely applied to faith. People can maintain faith without following a strict set of rules or guidelines.

President Barack Obama also shed light on this issue, based on his realization that all faith is not the same. Andre C. Willis (2008) notes the following:

> Obama will be a Christian pluralist. While his own conversion roots him firmly in the Christian faith, his intellectual skills and international experience allow him to understand that there are many paths to the truth. And his rhetorical abilities allow him to give new meaning to the language of faith to both positively affirm people of different faiths all over the world and properly acknowledge leaders from non-Christian nations.

Those searching for the absolute meaning of faith might be left with more questions than answers. It's that simple…because it's so complex.

All or Nothing

Another great debate about faith is the degree to which one believes. Must people completely believe in a higher power in order to be considered *faith-based* individuals, or can they lean toward a somewhat agnostic point of view? In other words, are people only classified as believers and non-believers, or can there be a gray area?

Obviously, true atheists do not find comfort in any type of spiritual source. They do not believe what they cannot see. For these people, faith is not there...and might not ever be there. So be it! This is their choice, and they have every right to feel this way. Non-atheists, on the other hand, might find gray area because they make mistakes. They have good days and bad days depending on the experiences life brings them. They are inconsistent about many things, so why should faith be different? Uncertainty brings about questions, and sometimes those questions are answered through some type of spiritual guidance.

One concern with those who are unsure involves the convenient agnostics who use faith as an ace in the hole. They want to be able to use it, but only if and when they need it. They feel that if there is some type of afterlife, they want to be able to get there by relying on the faith that was buried beneath the surface during their existence on earth. This is like buying a stock that can't go down in value. If it remains the same, then nothing is lost. If it goes up, then the rewards are reaped. The problem with such an investment is that it likely does not exist...similar to the faith of the convenient agnostic.

Faith Helps People View Negative Happenings Positively

One of the best things about faith is that it helps people forgive. While religion has undeniably been the root cause of many conflicts, faith helps heal others. *Turn the other cheek, forgive thy neighbor, reject hatred,* and *pray for sinners* are all examples of establishing positive viewpoints in the face of negative happenings through faith…and faith does not necessarily mean that everyone has to believe in the same higher being.

Christians, Muslims, Jewish, and Sikhs differ in their religious beliefs, but they are able to remain upbeat despite their circumstances due to their faith. For example, in June of 2008 a teenager had his arm bitten off and swallowed by an alligator while swimming in Florida. He believes God helped him on that tragic day because the detachment of his arm saved him from drowning (the alligator could have taken his life instead of just his arm). His Christian faith kept him upbeat during and after the attack, and allowed him to be thankful instead of bitter (TEEN WHO LOST ARM, 2008).

Anger is a negative reaction that poses many challenges. Everyone gets angry at some time, and controlling this can be an arduous task in certain situations. Lack of control can lead to devastating circumstances. Faith helps some people take a positive approach to anger management. Islam shed some light on this topic when Muhammad the Prophet stated the following:

> Powerful is not he who knocks the other down, indeed powerful is he who controls himself in a fit of anger (UNDERSTANDING ISLAM AND MUSLIMS, 1989).

The Sikhs tend to view all things in life positively. *Chardi Kala* is used in Sikhism to stress that Sikhs always remain positive. Being happy, staying cheerful, progressing always, keeping in high spirits, and remaining optimistic are all parts of this mental condition. This positive attitude teaches people to believe that they should not despair because they cannot be defeated by evil forces. This thinking is also extended to non-Sikhs by helping them achieve this same state of mind as they progress through the ups and downs of life.

Faith plays a role in helping those who are depressed. It might not be the sole solution for people experiencing depression, but it helps them view the resulting negatives in a more positive light. On the website selfgrowth.com, Dave Turo-Shields (2007) talks about reaching for a higher power that can be utilized as a positive resource. He posts the following about how faith helps people battle depression:

> I'm not preaching God or a Higher Power as the ONE and ONLY answer...I am simply hoping to get your attention for a moment. Belief in something bigger than you is one powerful resource that you can tap into this very moment. When added to the many other available depression support resources...you'll become unstoppable in your recovery.

Faith and its relationship to optimistic perception also extend into areas such as health care. A study by the University of Chicago (STUDY, 2007) found that the majority of doctors in the United States believe that people's spiritual faith aids them in viewing their personal health issues in a more positive light. This positive focus ultimately helps patients during the healing process. Even more interesting is the finding that only one percent of doctors believe that faith negatively influences their patients' health.

Faith also helps those experiencing normal bumps in the road during everyday life. Things do not always go exactly as planned, and little detours and distractions can be made easier for those believing in a higher power. People note that their faith helps them find solace after a hard day, stressful encounter, or mundane occurrence. Why is this the case? Because some people need a boost from something outside of the earthly resources they have readily available...and faith addresses that need quite well. Faith changes perception, and perception is reality.

A particularly dismal perception can be established when people are involved in war. The seemingly senseless atrocities that occur all around can create a desperate situation that is not easy to overcome. Faith can help here because it eases daily struggles while helping soldiers focus on coping with the realities of war. In Iraq, for example, Van Marsh (2007) found that the spiritual faith of Jewish, Muslim, and Christian American soldiers helped them remain upbeat during their deployment. This is a clear example of taking a positive view of something with obvious negatives.

Faith Improves Attitude

Everyone faces challenging issues that can influence happiness in their lives. The degree of happiness they experience is often not based on actual situations, but rather on their perception of those situations. Perception is reality, and that reality can lead to positive or negative thinking. For example, a woman might be going through a divorce after a mostly bad marriage. She can perceive this as the end of the world because she failed at marriage and has to start all over again, or she can view it as a fresh start after a relationship that was simply not right for either person.

Positive thinking helps people progress, while negative thinking leaves them in a rut that can be difficult to get out of…even to the point where they become withdrawn or depressed. Faith helps people think positively and find happiness because they believe they have spiritual guidance for problem resolution. It helps them understand the why things happen and become more appreciative and thankful for the good things that transpire. In short, faith helps people develop an *attitude of gratitude.*

Faith Teaches Patience

Patience is truly a virtue…and not everyone possesses that virtue. Many people search for immediate gratification which can lead to problems because good things often take time to transpire. Impatience results when people are unwilling or unable to wait out that time.

Maria T. Russell (2007) discusses the different faces of impatience. Sometimes people are impatient waiting for something to begin, such as a promotion to a higher position, and other times they are impatient waiting for something to end, such as the remodeling of a house. People are impatient because they are not satisfied with the present and cannot resist looking toward the future. This is not all bad because they visualize something better for themselves. However, they should not sacrifice the present because they have a vision of what could or should be in the future.

Russell makes the following astute observation about people's patience or lack of with each other:

> Another instance where patience is often sorely lacking is when dealing with our fellow human beings (and with ourselves). We get impatient because someone is "slow," "stupid," "opinionated," "stubborn," "addicted," "arrogant," etc. We let our impatience turn into judgment and anger, and we create mini-wars within our families, our workplace, our neighborhood. We let our impatience with the way things are be a cause of division between ourselves and others (2007).

Faith helps people realize that the things they yearn for do not have to happen immediately...in fact, it is sometimes best if they do not. Jim Long (1998) notes that God gives people the power to be patient in all situations and accept the present while waiting for change:

> We struggle with patience because we don't like the circumstances we face. Patience is difficult because things feel out of control. The timing seems wrong; the wait drags on and on. And yet, because God is in control, we *can* be patient...Because God's wisdom is flawless, we can wait...When we want circumstances to change, we wait for God to change those circumstances – or help us to change them. Or help us to accept whatever circumstances we're in. (Long, 1998)

Patience can also be learned through religious channels. Taoism exemplifies this well. While this doctrine is sometimes thought of as a mix of philosophy and psychology, it is considered a religious faith. Essentially, Taoists believe in finding truth by being patient and looking for natural patterns. They reject intolerance, violence, and hatred. They welcome love, learning, and harmony because these are taught by nature. They trust their lives in the Tao, so that they may live a balanced and peaceful mortal life and afterlife with the universe (REFORM TAOIST CONGREGATION, 2007).

When given time, faith guides and provides. It provides help for those in need of patience. This is reassuring because those who cannot wait sometimes end up without.

Faith Fosters Hope

Hope can be deceiving, but it is essential for many people. Without it, they are left feeling they have little reason to move past everyday challenges. Hope is a motivator for navigating through life's rough waters, and faith plays a major role here because it helps people look past difficult situations toward something better. The International AIDS Society (2008) at the Faith-Based Organizations Meeting noted that undying faith provides people with the strength to move forward, helps them in dire circumstances, and offers hope that the future will be better.

Faith helps bring hope to people facing harsh realities. After a tornado devastated Orlando, Florida, in early 2007, Lundy and Roberts (2007) reported that residents from the most devastated areas took time to pray together for their neighbors who perished. These individuals considered themselves fortunate for surviving the crisis and being able to move forward. They found the strength to continue on after losing loved ones and personal possessions. Their support for each other worked, and faith was at the core of that support.

Some people find solace in faith when facing the death of loved ones. Over half of the people surveyed in 2005 believed dying patients could be revived through divine intervention even if doctors believed that medical treatment was futile (GOD VS. DOCTOR, 2008). This indicates the power of faith is greater than faith in modern medical thinking. Faith offers hope in what are considered hopeless situations.

Faith also offers hope to those who have limited resources in times of need. Ex-offenders, for example, may find that they have very little support once they are released from prison. The loneliness and isolation these individuals experience can lead them back into the same lifestyle that landed them in jail in the first place. Ex-offenders who are also substance abusers face even a greater risk because mind-altering drugs seem to offer an escape from the problems at hand. They need support that does not exist, so they turn to their former addictions. Faith-based groups offer a new starting point for some ex-prisoners through discussion groups and spiritual counseling. Basic necessities, such as food, shelter, and transportation, are also provided to help these people remain sober and become independent (FAITH-BASED GROUPS HELP, 2003).

Friends and family provide a framework of support in troubling times. However, sometimes this support is not enough when life becomes problematic, so many people seek a higher source for solutions. Quite simply, faith helps those in difficult situations.

Faith Cultivates Compassion

Why aren't people always compassionate? The answer is fairly complex, but one major reason is that they simply find it unnecessary. This is especially true if the compassion they need to display does not agree with their personal beliefs or experiences. For example, people who have worked hard to educate themselves and fight their way out of poverty might find it difficult to have compassion for people who are poor, but, in their view, have done little to change their situations.

Lack of compassion can also occur within religion. People are not necessarily compassionate just because they are affiliated with some religious organization. Karen Armstrong notes the following about compassion and religion (Bistrich, 2007):

> Compassion is not a popular virtue. Many religious people prefer to be right rather than compassionate. They don't want to give up their egos. They want religion to give them a little mild uplift once a week so that they can return to their ordinary selfish lives, unscathed by the demands of their tradition. Religion is hard work; not many people do it well.

Armstrong's thoughts are compelling and interesting since many people of faith might think the opposite. However, she goes on to state (Bistrich, 2007):

> But are secularists any better? Many secularists would subscribe to the compassionate ideal but are just as selfish as religious people. The failure of religious people to be

compassionate doesn't tell us something about religion but about human nature. Religion is a method: you have to put it into practice to discover its truth. Not many people do, unfortunately.

Although some religious people may not appear to be compassionate, many others are quite the opposite. People from all nations have physical, mental, and spiritual needs that can only be met with the aid of others. Humanitarian efforts help here…and these efforts are often brought about by people of faith. In 2007, the Pew Forum's U.S. Religious Landscape Survey asked 35,000 adults about the impact of religion on society. They found that all religions support an increase in government assistance to the poor, regardless of debt incurred (RELIGIOUS AMERICANS: MY FAITH, 2008).

Followers of Hinduism promote compassion. Dharma, religious ethics put forth in ancient Indian scriptures by Hindu gurus, is partially rooted in kindness and empathy. Hindus believe that life should be lived according to Dharma in order to achieve good actions of body and mind, and compassion plays an important role.

Jewish people demonstrate compassion based on their faith. Jewish scholar and philosopher Moses Maimonides highlighted eight different levels of charity as follows (Sears, 1998):

1. One who gives unwillingly.
2. One who gives cheerfully, but not enough.
3. One who gives enough, but not till he is asked.
4. One who gives before being asked, but directly to the poor person.
5. The poor one knows from whom he or she takes, but the giver does not know who is receiving.
6. The giver knows to whom he or she gives, but the receiver does not know the giver.
7. The giver does not know to whom he or she gives, nor does the poor person know from whom he or she receives.

8. The highest form of charity is to strengthen the hand of the poor by giving a loan, or joining in partnership, or training out of the individual's poverty, to help become independent. The highest level of charity – helping a person establish herself or himself – is the foremost ideal of our modern social agenda as we address the complex issues of poverty and welfare and seek the best ways to help people break the chains of poverty.

The higher levels of charity outlined by Maimonides demonstrate the compassion of Judaism and indicate the willingness of Jewish people to make the world a better place.

Shinto, an ancient Japanese religion, has no authentic founder and no documented or written scriptures. It operates with a loosely organized priesthood and has no actual form of religious law, but followers believe in helping others without the thought of material or personal gain. According to the Shinto webpage of religious tolerance (RELIGIONS OF THE WORLD, 2007), the Association of Shinto Shrines urges members to help others through good deeds without expecting rewards.

People of the Methodist faith reach out to those who are feeling lost or find themselves in disparaging situations. They indicate that their mission is to listen to people, accept their problems, and invite them into the family of faith (Koehler, 2006).

People from a wide variety of religious backgrounds are compassionate and help others based upon their viewpoints…and those viewpoints are often established from their faith. Faith does not call upon those who are qualified; it qualifies those who are called.

Faith Encourages Persistence

People often need strength to keep going as they encounter life's challenges. They lose focus of previously established goals when those challenges, no matter how big or small, seem insurmountable. This results in giving up and moving in another direction.

President John F. Kennedy began the United States' journey as the first nation to land a man on the moon. He encountered many challenges, but did not let these distract him in his efforts. Many people doubted him and his actions, but his faith kept him moving forward…and his persistence paid off in less than 10 years.

Martin Luther King, Jr. maintained his course of action despite life threatening circumstances. Zaleski and Doto (2007), on the First Unitarian Church of Portland website, describe his actions during the Montgomery bus boycott that sparked the United States Civil Rights Movement. In a nutshell, Rosa Parks, an African American, refused to move to the back of the bus so a white man could have her seat. She was ultimately arrested, and this caused King and other black leaders to organize the boycott. Within weeks, white city officials began harassing King and labeled him the main problem to any type of resolution. He received many threatening phone calls, but one in particular on the night of January 27, 1956, left him in a panic mode. He was afraid his family might be killed and contemplated quitting the Civil Rights Movement. He could not sleep as he tried to think of a way out of the movement without appearing weak or afraid. After believing he had nowhere left to turn, he found his answer in prayer. He experienced the presence of the Divine, who told him not to be afraid and to stand up for what was right. From that point on he was committed to achieving civil rights using nonviolent methods.

People with faith are often more persistent than those without because they experience less negative emotions. Fear, stress, and anxiety are less likely to surface because faith brings about relaxation. Adebola A. Oni (2006) indicated that a state of absolute faith brings about a feeling that all challenges can be overcome. Staying on track is less difficult, and obstacles come to be viewed as part of the perfection process. Strong faith allows believers to become unmoved when confronted with problems, so solutions can be seen more clearly.

Faith helps people stay on track as they strive to reach new levels of accomplishment. Hard work is the ship that takes people to their destination, but faith is the compass that keeps it from drifting off course.

Faith Brings About Inner Peace

Inner peace should not be underestimated because it is critical for achieving balance in life. If a person is not happy with him or herself, he or she will likely find difficulty being happy with others. Faith plays a role here because many people have reported finding an inner peace due to their religious experiences. Inner peace is described as being obtained through faith (The Albuquerque Buddhist Fellowship Group):

> Without attaining inner peace there can be no world peace. In order to establish peace, freedom from war and conflict, whether personal or social, we have first to establish an inner peace that we must then sustain in our daily lives. For world peace to be achieved, individuals must attain inner peace. This is a basic principle of Buddhism.
>
> In the Buddhist tradition there are various ways of realizing this inner peace, from the gradual purification of the mind found in Theravada Buddhism to the sudden awakening to one's original nature that typifies Zen. How then do we Shin Buddhists achieve this inner peace? The answer is simple: through attainment of faith in Amida Buddha (Albuquerque Buddhist Fellowship Group, 2001).

Islam also promotes inner peace. Although branded by western media as terrorists in recent years, it is not fair to blame all those associated with the religion of Islam for the violent activities of those calling themselves Muslims. This is like saying that Catholics promote terrorism based on certain past actions of the Irish Republican Army. Sayyid Muhammad Rizvi (n.d.) notes the following:

Muslims often greet each other by saying "salamun alaykum – peace be upon you." The daily prayers also end with the same sentence. In Islam, one of the names by which God is known is "Salam" which means peace. A person can achieve inner peace by creating harmony and balance between his main emotions (desire and anger) and his spiritual self. In other words, between his emotions and his conscience.

Judaism is also a contributor to inner peace because it provides an understanding of the daily turmoil experienced by people. Jewish individuals facing everyday ups and downs can find inner peace based on their faith that is not achievable elsewhere. According to Rabbi Aron Moss (2004):

> Some of us have been taught that we should seek inner peace and serenity. Some even claim to have reached it. You can experience a temporary serenity by ignoring the voice of either the body or the soul – either by indulging in materialism or escaping to a spiritual oasis. But our other side will eventually assert itself. As long as we inhabit this earth, our bodies and souls are bound to each other. We can become "spiritual," but our bodily cravings will not disappear; we can become materialistic, but our soul's yearning will not be quieted.
>
> Judaism offers a different path. The Kabbalists taught that the soul was sent down to this world not to avoid the body, but to teach it. The focus of Jewish spirituality is refining our worldly self – our bodily cravings, our character, our lifestyle. This is not achieved by escaping the body/soul tension, but rather by embracing that tension. Enjoy the pleasures of this world, but don't become trapped in them. Seek spirituality, but don't lose your personality.

Essentially, Rabbi Moss goes on to say that the Torah does not guarantee a path to inner peace. It does, however, bring meaning to the stress and problems that encompass life, and it purifies the struggle to overcome these issues. This is by no means the simplest path because it entails living on the edge of spirituality and materialism…but life is true to the body and soul.

As noted earlier, faith fosters hope when people face death situations. Along the same lines, one of the greatest ways faith brings about inner peace is after the passing of a family member or close acquaintance. The familiar statement "he is in a better place now" exemplifies people's spiritual beliefs. They believe the deceased has left this earthly world and moved on to a better one…and this makes them feel better for that person and for themselves.

Faith helps people bring closure to death situations so they are able to move forward and face the challenges that confront their everyday lives. It also comforts them in believing that they will someday reunite with the deceased in some type of eternal bliss. They believe in an afterlife because they can see it using their faith.

Inner peace is best achieved when people understand and accept why things happen. Faith helps establish the understanding that leads to the acceptance.

Faith Promotes Forgiving

The road to forgiving others is often a difficult one. Some people simply do not want to forgive…so they do not. Others have the desire, but simply cannot release the negative feelings trapped inside. Still others claim to forgive, but their inability to forget continually resurfaces the negative emotions that prevented them from forgiving in the first place…and the end result is unhappiness.

The concept of forgiving is interesting because adults often find it more difficult to forgive than children. Children can be cruel to each other, and then be back to playing together within minutes. They tend to quickly forgive others for their mean actions, even though the situation seemed to be of the utmost importance as it transpired. As children mature into adults, they generally become more sensitive to the feelings of others. They are less likely to be callous toward other people out of respect. However, if they do offend or hurt other people, their actions can cause pain that lingers for quite some time. Family members might not talk to each other for years, possibly even never again, based on a disagreement that occurred; friendships can be strained to the point where they break or are never the same. Essentially, children might not be as courteous as adults, but they find it easier to forgive when they believe they have been mistreated.

Faith helps people forgive by giving them the strength to move forward. Through spiritual belief, negative feelings are confronted and better understood…and the result is a happier self. Actress Mia Farrow exemplified this when she used her Catholic faith to come to terms with the fact that her then husband, Woody Allen, fell in love and later married her adopted daughter, Soon-Yi Previn:

> My faith has helped me through many difficult times.
> It made me understand what it is by that which cannot
> be taken away. The essential self that is yours and yours
> alone cannot be taken away. Only you can give it up.
> Things can be taken away and that can be painful. Loss is
> painful (Pringle, 2006).

Farrow was then asked if she had forgiven Allen for his actions. Her response was as follows:

> In an instant. I can't carry any of that. That's too heavy for
> me. It really isn't up to me to forgive or not forgive, is it
> (Pringle, 2006)?

Farrow's faith took the burden of decision-making off her shoulders. She might not have been able to forget, but she did forgive…and this made moving forward with her life a little easier.

One of the greatest examples of faith-inspired forgiving involves the Amish. The following is an account of the tragedy that transpired and was ultimately forgiven in Lancaster County, Pennsylvania, on October 2, 2006 (TRAGIC SHOOTING AT AN AMISH SCHOOL, 2008):

> Charlie Roberts was a milk truck driver who serviced
> the local community, including the farms of some of
> the victims' families. Nine years earlier his wife Amy
> gave birth to their first child, a baby girl. However, the
> baby died after living only 20 minutes. Apparently his
> daughter's death affected him greatly. He never forgave
> God for her death, and eventually planned to get revenge.
>
> On the morning of October 2nd Roberts said goodbye to
> two of his own children at the school bus stop, then drove
> to the West Nickel Mines Amish School. When he walked
> in the door, some of the children recognized him. That day
> the school had four adult visitors – the teacher's mother,
> her sister, and two sisters-in-law. One of the women was
> pregnant. When the young teacher saw his guns, she and

her mother left the other adults with the children and ran to a nearby house for help. A call was made to 911.

The pregnant visitor was trying to comfort 7-year-old Naomi Rose when Roberts ordered the adults to leave. Then he told the boys to leave. The boys huddled near an outhouse to pray. Roberts had the 10 girls lie down facing the blackboard and he tied their hands and feet. Roberts told the girls he was sorry for what he was about to do, but "I'm angry at God and I need to punish some Christian girls to get even with him."

When the state police arrived, Roberts ordered them to leave the property or he would shoot. He told the girls, "I'm going to make you pay for my daughter." One of the girls, 13-year-old Marian, said, "Shoot me first." Roberts began shooting each of the girls before finally shooting himself. When the police broke in to the school, two of the girls, including Marian, were dead. Naomi Rose died in the arms of a state trooper.

While this type of heinous and senseless crime might seem inexcusable to many, it was thought of differently by the Amish. They chose to forgive, and did not point a finger at anyone. They did not hire attorneys to file a lawsuit, nor did they hold a press conference to express their anger or pain. Instead they showed empathy and compassion toward the family of the man who took the lives of innocent children. They visited Robert's family, on the day of the shooting, to comfort them in their sorrow. The Roberts family was invited to the funeral of one of the Amish girls, and there were more Amish than non-Amish mourners at the killer's funeral. Despite Robert's actions, a grandfather of one of the girls killed expressed forgiveness for him (AMISH FORGIVENESS, 2008).

This story is truly amazing. The actions and words of the Amish involved are inspirational to any person of faith…and any person, for that matter.

People who cannot forgive often die with bitterness toward others. Forgiving is essential if people want to progress through life in a positive manner. The process can be painful and difficult, but it can be facilitated using faith.

Faith Encourages Mutual Respect

Hindus believe people should not behave toward others in ways that are not agreeable with what they themselves believe.

Christianity preaches "loving thy neighbor as thyself."

The Anglican Church places great emphasis on theological exploration from a Christian perspective. Based on this thinking, it is not surprising that they believe in mutual respect for others. This is demonstrated by their emphasis on the doctrines of Creation and the Incarnation (Bays, 1996).

> We affirm that the world and human beings are good because they are God's creation. In Jesus Christ, God became human and shared in our everyday existence. God must value human nature very highly if God is willing, in Jesus Christ, to "take our nature upon him" as our prayers say. And if God also raises that same human nature to new life after Jesus endured suffering and death. We must work to bring all of humanity to its full potential as God intended, and I rejoice that we do this by loving God and by being involved in our society to work for change.

Confucians believe that they should not do to others what they do not want done to themselves.

Jainism definitely encourages mutual respect. Basically known as an Indian religion of love and compassion, the Jains believe the universe is eternal, and they also believe in the eternity of the soul. They preach respect for all life, even showing consideration for animals (JAINISM, n.d.).

Lord Mahavira is regarded as a reformer and propagator of

Jainism. He is considered to be the last of a line of 24 holy and spiritually enlightened beings, the Tirthankaras; and he gave up his life as a wealthy prince to devote himself to the religion (JAINISM, n.d.).

Followers of Jainism do not necessarily promote belief in a creator God, but they are faith-based. Five great vows include the following (JAINISM, n.d.):

- *Nonviolence* (Ahimsa) not to cause harm to any living beings
- *Truthfulness* (Satya) to speak the harmless truth only
- *Non-stealing* (Asteya) not to take anything not properly given
- *Chastity* (Brahmacharya) not to indulge in sensual pleasure
- *Non-possession/Non-attachment* (Aparigraha) complete detachment from people, places, and material things

In 1975, the Jains decided on an open palm as a symbol to symbolize non-violence…and ultimately respect for the beliefs of others. This was done in 1975 because it was the 2500th anniversary of Lord Mahavira's enlightenment.

Shamanism is a non-traditional religion that also encourages respect for others. According to their creed (SHAMAN'S CREED, 2008):

> We believe there are other Dimensions co-existing with and through our own, and that other-Dimension Beings can and do have a direct and profound Effect on us, especially when we do not know of their Existence. We therefore believe all Things and Times are intricately related and of equal spiritual Importance, and so we honor all of Creation as we honor Ourselves.

Shamans believe all things have a sacred reason for being. This thinking encourages appreciation of the diversity that others bring to this planet.

Another example of faith encouraging mutual respect lies within Congregationalism. The followers of this particular religion are tolerant of others…and they are also tolerant of themselves.

To clarify here, Congregationalists believe it is the right and responsibility of each congregation in the denomination to independently operate itself. Governing decisions are made within each individual establishment, and there is no upper management that dictates rules and bylaws. Even more interesting is the fact that the autonomous principles of the Congregationalists have been adopted by the Unitarian Universalist Association and some Jewish Synagogues.

The world would most likely be a better place if people had one hundred percent mutual respect for one another. While this is probably not attainable, everyone can work harder at treating others the way they would prefer to be treated…and faith can be their guiding light.

Faith Inspires People

Many musicians write about God based on their religious upbringings. Obviously, gospel and Christian singers fall into this category, but U2 is a world famous rock band with Christian ties. This is apparent as they acknowledge their faith in certain songs, some of which went on to become hit records.

Bono, lead singer of U2, does not tie himself to any particular organized religion. As noted by Kevin Eckstrom (2006):

> For one, Bono brings his own personal faith to bear, one that is deeply personal and not necessarily shaped by the four walls of the church. He finds hope in Jesus' Sermon on the Mount, inspiration in the Hebrew prophets and solace in the idea of undeserved grace.

Country legend Johnny Cash also utilizes faith in his music. His words reached millions and made him a household name, outselling even the Beatles in 1969. Cash battled drug and alcohol dependency during his career and health problems toward the end of his life, but this did not deter him from the faith he obtained after listening to a Baptist sermon with his wife, June Carter Cash (Curry, 2003).

In a 1992 interview with Larry King, Cash was asked if he was bitter with God and replied:

> No, I'm not bitter. Why should I be bitter? I'm thrilled to death with life. Life is – the way God has given it to me was just a platter – a golden platter of life laid out there for me. It's been beautiful (Curry, 2003).

Athletes find faith essential in many instances. Some indicate they find strength through a belief in a higher power that helps them succeed in challenging situations. Three time Super Bowl quarterback Kurt Warner had this to say about his faith (Kriegel, 2009):

> It's an advantage for any individual, when you have faith and believe in something. I walk by faith and not by sight. I walk according to what I believe, and what I believe the power of God is, as opposed to what the world tells us, or what circumstances appear to be. So much of this business is 'me, me me'... my faith has allowed me to step back from that and say, 'hey, this isn't about me.'

The most interesting aspect about Warner is the fact that he was considered washed up years before his 2009 Super Bowl appearance. He was let go by two NFL teams and was not even named to the starting position for the 2008 season. He credits his faith for his ability to overcome doubters and beat incredible odds.

NFL writer Mark Kriegel is not a believer that God determines outcomes of football games. In his column he states (Kriegel, 2009):

> Personally, my own taste in quarterbacks runs toward the epic old-school debauchers, guys like Kenny Stabler and Joe Namath. If I go to Hell for that, then so be it. I refuse to believe that God – *anyone's* God – has a rooting interest in the outcome of something as secular and perverse as a BCS game.

Although Kriegel (2009) admonishes the importance of God and religion in sports, he does not reduce the significance of faith. He later admits that it plays a role on the field…and that faith can be spiritual:

> Actually, the issue isn't really religion. It's faith. I don't care what or whom a ballplayer believes in: Jesus, Moses, Buddha, L. Ron Hubbard. I don't care what his position is on stem cell research, abortion, gay rights. But a system of belief – any system, really – that stills the mind and quells doubt is of obvious benefit, particularly if you're an athlete.

Actors also benefit from their faith. Danny Thomas founded St. Jude Children's Research Hospital based on his faith. His amazing story is found on the St. Jude Children's Hospital website (St. Jude Children's Research, 2008):

> More than 70 years ago, Danny Thomas, then a struggling young entertainer with a baby on the way, visited a Detroit church. He was so moved during the Mass that he placed his last $7 in the collection box. He prayed for a way to pay the looming hospital bills. The next day, he was offered a small part that would pay 10 times the amount he'd given to the church.
>
> Two years later, Danny Thomas had achieved moderate acting success in Detroit, but he was struggling to take his career to the next level. Once again, he turned to the church. Praying to St. Jude Thaddeus, the patron saint of hopeless causes, Danny Thomas asked the saint to "help me find my way in life, and I will build you a shrine."
>
> In the years that followed, Danny Thomas' career flourished through films and television, and he became an internationally known entertainer. He remembered his pledge to build a shrine to St. Jude.
>
> In the early 1950s, Danny Thomas began discussing with friends what concrete form his vow might take. Thomas and a group of Memphis, Tennessee businessmen who had agreed to help support his dream seized on the idea of creating a unique research hospital devoted to curing catastrophic diseases in children. More than just a treatment facility, this would be a research center for the children of the world.
>
> By 1955, the local business leaders who had joined his cause began area fundraising efforts, supplementing Danny Thomas' benefit shows that brought scores of major entertainment stars to Memphis. Danny Thomas

crisscrossed the United States by car talking about his dream and raising funds at meetings and benefits. Although Danny Thomas and his friends raised the money to build the hospital, they now faced the daunting task of funding its annual operation.

To solve this problem, Danny Thomas turned to his fellow Americans of Arabic-speaking heritage. His request struck a responsive chord. In 1957, 100 representatives of the Arab-American community met in Chicago to form ALSAC® with a sole purpose of raising funds for the support of St. Jude Children's Research Hospital.

Since that time, with national headquarters in Memphis and regional offices throughout the United States, ALSAC has assumed full responsibility for all the hospital's fundraising efforts, raising hundreds of millions annually through benefits and solicitation drives among Americans of all ethnic, religious and racial backgrounds. Today, ALSAC is the nation's second largest health-care charity and is supported by the efforts of more than 1 million volunteers nationwide.

The work of Danny Thomas and the people at the St. Jude Children's Research Hospital inspired the writing of this book and, as a result, ten percent of all sales will be donated to the hospital's research. Essentially, St. Jude reflects people's ability to utilize their faith to overcome the seemingly impossible situations they encounter in everyday life. Faith truly does inspire those who believe!

Faith Helps Resolve Conflict

War can be, and has been, a direct result of religion. Modern day examples of this include (1) Protestant and Catholic and (2) Jewish and Muslim. Why does this happen? That question might never be completely answered, but the Religious Tolerance website gives a list of the factors that are partially involved (RELIGIOUSLY MOTIVATED VIOLENCE, 2006):

- Many people are motivated to adopt a religious faith out of a need for security in a dangerous world. When their religion is challenged, they react emotionally and sometimes violently.

- Many people believe that there is only *one* "top-down" religion: i.e. there is only a single religion revealed by God to humanity. That sole religion is, of course, their own. Meanwhile they believe that *all* other religions are "bottom-up" faiths: i.e. religions created by humans to express their concept of God. It is difficult for a person to respect other religions if they "know" that their religion, alone, is the true one.

- Many feel that they are God's only representatives on Earth; in effect, they are God's arms and legs. They feel a need to be God's defenders.

The above list paints a fairly bleak picture since there is no quick or permanent fix to a problem that has existed for centuries. However, although war is sometimes caused by religious doctrine, faith also has the ability to bring about conflict resolution. People sometimes use their faith to make decisions that bring about peace, as exemplified by *The Geneva Spiritual Appeal*, signed on October 24, 1999.

The Geneva Spiritual Appeal took place in Geneva, Switzerland. This meeting involved leaders from Christian (Old Catholic, Roman Catholic, Orthodox, and Protestant), Buddhist, Jewish and Muslim religions. The main focal point of this gathering was to look at religion as a major cause of violence…which differed from past religious meetings that focused on reducing human suffering that resulted from conflict. The result was the signing of *The Geneva Spiritual Appeal*. This document asked religious leaders to guarantee that their faiths were not used to justify future violence. In short, those signing agreed to adhere to the following three principles (GENEVA SPIRITUAL APPEAL, 2003):

1. Refusal to invoke a religious or spiritual power to justify violence of any kind
2. Refusal to invoke a religious or spiritual source to justify discrimination and exclusion
3. Refusal to exploit or dominate others by means of strength, intellectual capacity or spiritual persuasion, wealth or social status

Other hope for conflict resolution among those of differing faiths can be seen in their shared belief that people should treat others the way they would like to be treated. This common ground is known as the *ethics of reciprocity*. The following passages are from the religious texts of various secular beliefs, religions, and faiths as posted on the Religious Tolerance website (SHARED BELIEF IN THE, 2006):

- Brahmanism:
  - "This is the sum of Dharma [duty]: Do naught unto others which would cause you pain if done to you." Mahabharata, 5:1517
- Buddhism:
  - "Hurt not others in ways that you yourself would find hurtful." Udana-Varga 5:18

- Christianity:
  - "And as ye would that men should do to you, do ye also to them likewise." Luke 6:31, King James Version
- Confucianism:
  - "Do not do to others what you do not want them to do to you." Analects 15:23
- Ancient Egyptian:
  - "Do for one who may do for you, that you may cause him thus to do." The Tale of the Eloquent Peasant, 109–110 Translated by R.B. Parkinson.
- Hinduism:
  - "This is the sum of duty: do not do to others what would cause pain if done to you." Mahabharata 5:1517
- Islam:
  - "None of you [truly] believes until he wishes for his brother what he wishes for himself." Number 13 of Imam "Al-Nawawi's Forty Hadiths"
- Jainism:
  - "In happiness and suffering, in joy and grief, we should regard all creatures as we regard our own self." Lord Mahavira, 24th Tirthankara
- Judaism:
  - "...thou shalt love thy neighbor as thyself." Leviticus 19:18
- Native American Spirituality:
  - "Respect for all life is the foundation." The Great Law of Peace
- Shinto:
  - "Be charitable to all beings, love is the representative of God." Ko-ji-ki Hachiman Kasuga

- Sikhism:
    - "No one is my enemy, none a stranger and everyone is my friend." Guru Arjan Dev: AG 1299
- Sufism:
    - "The basis of Sufism is consideration of the hearts and feelings of others." Dr. Javad Nurbakhsh, Master of the Nimatullahi Sufi Order
- Taoism:
    - "Regard your neighbor's gain as your own gain, and your neighbor's loss as your own loss." T'ai Shang Kan Ying P'ien
- Unitarian:
    - "We affirm and worth and dignity of every person."
- Zoroastrianism:
    - "Whatever is disagreeable to yourself do not do unto others." Shayast-na-Shayast 13:29

Faith might be a cause of some conflicts, but it also can be a solution for others.

Faith Promotes Tolerance of Other Religions

Tolerance is a very interesting topic. For example, look at typical non-conformists. These are people who disagree with those who conform to status quo thinking. They believe things should change, are vocal about their ideas, and often have legitimate arguments to support their thinking. These same people, however, can be very intolerant of other non-conformists who do not conform to their idea of non-conformity. How can this be? The reason is simple. They see only what they want to see, and other viewpoints do not meet this criterion.

Tolerance can be challenging when dealing with people who only see what they want to see. Anyone who has had to listen to friends brag about the alleged accomplishments of their children can likely relate well to this statement. Again the reasoning is simple. People find it difficult to tolerate something they do not want to hear and are not certain they believe.

People are also intolerant of different forms of spirituality, but faith can help them accept the religious views of others. The Mormons exemplify this well due to the persecution experienced by the Church of Jesus Christ of Latter Day Saints in the early days. Religious intolerance at that time resulted in the suffering of these individuals. Now all church members, including missionaries, are expected to be respectful toward other beliefs. This is indicated in the eleventh of their Articles of Faith:

We claim the privilege of worshipping Almighty God

according to the dictates of our own conscience, and allow all men the same privilege, let them worship how, where, or what they may.

The BBC also notes the following on Mormonism (2008):

Mormons do not believe that they are the only people inspired by God and so have a tolerant attitude to other faiths. Although Mormons are certain that their Church teaches the true doctrines of salvation, they don't see it as the only teacher of truth. They believe that there is truth in many religions and philosophies, and that the teachings of many different great religious leaders have raised the spiritual and moral awareness of humanity. They see all human beings as children of the Father in heaven, regardless of their beliefs.

Islam has similar beliefs. Consider this information:

It is one function of Islamic law to protect the privileged status of minorities, and this is why non-Muslim places of worship have flourished all over the Islamic world. History provides many examples of Muslim tolerance towards other faiths: when the caliph Omar entered Jerusalem in the year 634, Islam granted freedom of worship to all religious communities in the city. Islamic law also permits non-Muslim minorities to set up their own courts, which implement family laws drawn up by the minorities themselves. (UNDERSTANDING ISLAM AND MUSLIMS, 1989)

Methodists desire to work with all religions to make the world a better place. An excerpt from The United Methodist Members Handbook (Koehler, 2006) states:

We cannot be effective in ministry on our own. So the congregation exists, in part, to surround and support each member in his or her ministry.

This excerpt shows an acceptance of other religions that

promotes tolerance of all faiths. It follows the same thinking as the Presbyterians, who strive to live in harmony with other faiths and acknowledge differing spiritual beliefs and motivations.

Jehovah's Witness followers also think along the same lines. An example of this occurred in Berlin, Germany, in the 1930s. According to an article on their website, the following happened after Hitler came into power (COURAGE IN THE FACE, 2008):

> It quickly became apparent that Jehovah's Witnesses were to be among the first targets of brutal Nazi suppression. The Witnesses were again branded as accomplices in an alleged Bolshevik-Jewish conspiracy. A campaign of persecution began. Why would such a small religious community attract the fury of the new regime? Historian Brian Dunn identifies three fundamental reasons: (1) the international scope of the Witnesses, (2) their opposition to racism, and (3) their position of neutrality toward the State. Because of their Scriptural views, the German Witnesses refused to give the Hitler salute, to support the National Socialist Party, or later on to participate in military activities. As a result, the Witnesses endured threats, interrogations, house searches, and other harassment by the police and SA.

Through all of this, the Witnesses recognized the right of others to worship as driven by their own thoughts and consciences. They believed in family values and religious freedom, stemming from their respect for all cultures and ethnic backgrounds.

Orthodox Christians are another faith-based group of people who preach tolerance of those who express religion differently. Their thinking is inspirational for those who believe in religious freedom (Papademetriou, 2009):

> Orthodox Christian people most often live in societies of cultural, linguistic and religious pluralism. For that reason, the Orthodox have developed an attitude of respect for others, and a tolerance and understanding for people of other faiths. The Orthodox Church does not have an

"official" pronouncement expressing the attitude toward other religions. However, Orthodoxy has a long-standing tradition showing respect and tolerance for people of other faiths. It is well-stated by an Orthodox Christian theologian and Archbishop, Anastasios Yannoulatos, of Albania, that, "being created in the image of God, every human being is our brother and sister."

It is a strong Orthodox view that our commitment to the Christian truth claim must affirm a pluralistic democratic setting for all people to live in peace and harmony. Orthodoxy holds fast to the truth of Christianity and defends the right of other religious expressions to co-exist in harmony in a democratic system where the law equally protects all.

An organization that encourages tolerance of other religious beliefs is the Interfaith Youth Core (IFYC). Young people of different faiths interact to make communities better while encouraging religious pluralism. This religious pluralism goes beyond tolerance for other religions. It is a situation where people share respect for each other's religious identities and develop working relationships that benefit those in need. Their goal is simple – make the world a better place. Their website states the following about what they do (Interfaith Youth Core, 2009):

> There are millions of religious young people in the world interacting with greater frequency. That interaction tends either toward conflict or cooperation. Where so many of these interactions tend towards conflict, the Interfaith Youth Core aims to introduce a new relationship, one that is about mutual respect and religious pluralism. Instead of focusing a dialogue on political or theological differences, we build relationships on the values that we share, such as hospitality and caring for the Earth, and how we can live out those values together to contribute to the betterment of our community.

It is fairly obvious from the work of the IFYC that faith can better things in this world...especially when there is freedom to express that faith in diverse ways.

Another interesting project related to religious tolerance involves a variety of different faiths coming together to defend the environment. Known as The Earth Healing Initiative, this group is composed of Roman Catholics, Episcopalians, Lutherans, Presbyterians, United Methodists, Unitarian Universalists, Baha'i, Jewish, The Religious Society of Friends (also known as the Quakers) and Zen Buddhists. They offer interfaith liaisons that encourage members of local churches and temples to participate in the Earth Day events. The differing faiths respect each other's beliefs while working together to protect the environment. One example is their effort to create a safe and effective habitat for bees since billions have died prematurely in recent years (Peterson, 2008).

It makes perfect sense that people of faith would tolerate those with differing religious viewpoints. After all, they all share a belief in a higher power...even though that higher power might not be the same in every case.

Faith-Based Organizations (FBO)

Money certainly does not guarantee happiness, but it is a known fact that lack of it can create misery. Based on this thinking, how much money is enough to prevent misery? That is a million dollar question that is very difficult to answer. However, some people truly have needs that are not met by the financial resources available to them. There are also those with mental, physical, and spiritual needs that cannot be met by their non-monetary resources.

Faith-based organizations play a critical role in helping those in need. Many people would perish from this earth without the aid of these entities simply because they have nowhere else to turn. AIDS, for example, is a viral infection that has killed over 25,000,000 people since 1981. This monster of a disease has no known cure, but a fight goes on to defeat it, and faith-based organizations are leading the way. Opening remarks at the Faith-Based Organization meeting (International AIDS Society, 2008) note the following in response to the AIDS epidemic facing the world:

> What we call "faith-based organizations" in the HIV response, the groups of people from various religious affiliations – whether the "great religions" of Christianity, Judaism, Islam, Hinduism, or Buddhism or smaller religions and spiritual groupings – have been active in the HIV response since the beginning of the epidemic. It is well-documented that a significant portion of HIV prevention, treatment, care and support is provided through faith-based organizations, to different degrees but substantial in all parts of the world. Particularly in the area of care and support,

many faith-based organizations have been at the frontline of the response to HIV since the very beginning and challenged those who were not. In the early years of the epidemic, some were the only groups willing to provide solace for the dying. When many others shunned those living with HIV/AIDS, many Christians and people from other religions reached out with compassion to those in their communities who were in need. In the era of increasing access to antiretroviral therapy, faith-based organizations throughout the world play a substantial role in delivering treatment and care to their communities. Increasingly, they are engaged in HIV prevention activities as well.

Also on the topic of AIDS, a report by the World Health Organization (WHO) found that faith-based organizations play a critical role in HIV/AIDS care and treatment in sub-Saharan Africa. This role is much greater than was previously thought before the research was conducted (World Health Organization, 2008).

The World Health Organization (2008) report argues:

> ...health, religion and cultural norms and values define the health-seeking strategies of many Africans. The failure of health policy makers to understand the overarching influence of religion – and the important role of FBOs in HIV treatment and care – could seriously undermine efforts to scale up health services.

This same report indicates the willingness of the World Health Organization to help resolve this issue by calling for increased communication between spiritual and public health leaders in the following areas:

- *Developing religious and public health literacy*: Formal courses, joint training and shared materials to improve understanding between FBOs and public health agencies.
- *Respectful engagement*: Expanding community workshops (as used in this study) to engage more FBOs in community

health work; and bringing together religious and public health leaders in "Executive Sessions" to encourage long-term collaboration in policy-making and project implementation.

- *Coordinating religious and health systems*: Extending the use of health mapping to identify FBOs that could help in scaling up services; strengthening community support groups and further linking them to nearby state-run hospitals, clinics, and dispensaries.

- *Further collaborative research*: Extending the participatory mapping used in this study to other African countries and low- and middle-income regions of the world; and further examining the nature of intangible (spiritual encouragement, knowledge, etc.) health assets revealed in this report.

As noted earlier, faith-based groups help ex-prisoners fight the demons that landed them in jail from re-occurring once they are released. Larger, more structured faith-based organizations fulfill a similar role (D'Amico, 2007):

> Faith-based institutions can offer a wealth of resources, services and ministries in the communities to which ex-inmates return. For many years, they have been involved in the work of helping ex-inmates and their families cope with the effects of incarceration and return. It is important to note that some of the most active and influential faith-based institutions are located in communities hardest hit by the cycle of imprisonment, release and reincarceration. Where traditional public and nonprofit programs may not be able to reach the most at-risk former inmates in poor communities, well-established churches and other faith-based institutions can fill this void with social, education and employment services.

There are some roadblocks for prisoners who might benefit from faith-based help. Understandably, government agencies are not allowed to encourage any particular religious organization, religion, sect, or other faith-based belief system. Additionally, parolees and probationers cannot be required to participate in any type of faith-based programs. Lastly, money can be a constraint since funding faith-based entities is often a challenge (D'Amico, 2007). Regardless of these obstacles, those who do find help here can benefit in many ways from the faith they develop or rediscover. Faith can bring comfort and solutions to many of their existing problems.

One of the best faith-based organizations that supports the premise of this book is the Tony Blair Faith Foundation. Started in May 2008 by Tony Blair, Prime Minister of Great Britain and Northern Ireland from May 1997 to June 2007, this foundation helps major faiths understand and accept each other. It works with all people including those in the Christian, Muslim, Jewish, Hindu, Sikh and Buddhist faiths.

One of the main objectives of Blair's organization is listed in the mission statement (Tony Blair Faith Foundation, 2008):

> Promote respect and understanding about the world's major religions and show how faith is a powerful force for good in the modern world.

The Tony Blair Faith Foundation's mission statement (2008) also talks about the importance of faith to millions of people worldwide. Faith brings people together, aids the less fortunate, and helps create mutual respect among all people. In short, it helps make the world a better place.

Although faith can make the world a better place, history has shown that it can also be a tool used to divide people and create hatred. The Tony Blair Faith Foundation (2008) responds to this type of challenge by educating and informing people about the differences among faiths of the world. The hope is to create empathy and understanding for people in all religions.

Additionally, the Tony Blair Faith Foundation (2008) encourages all people of faith to work together with the goal of eliminating as much global poverty and global conflict as possible. These inter-faith initiatives help illuminate the positive contributions and images of religions worldwide.

One of the current projects being worked on by the Tony Blair Faith Foundation is *Schools and Young People*. This project seeks to understand the role of faith in the modern world. Young people are asked to explore different faiths and help decrease the fear and tension associated with them. They are encouraged to submit their ideas and viewpoints for discussion. The ultimate goal is to reduce global religious intolerance in the new digital generation. The following is taken from the organization's website (Tony Blair Faith Foundation, 2008):

- First, we are creating a showcase of faith stories from around the world. As the world gets more global, religious literacy – the ability to understand the values of different faiths – will be increasingly important. Stories are the currency of human contact, through which we begin to understand each other and our world. So, whether a photo of your temple or synagogue, a video showing an Eid celebration, an activity that you organized to help your community, or perhaps a story that illustrates your views or experiences of other faith.

- Second, we are inviting young people (aged 10–16) to submit ideas for practical resources, materials and tools that might support inter-faith dialogue and exchange. You may have an idea for a specialist wikipedia, a strip cartoon, a radio program or a computer game. Whatever your idea, as long as it is designed to break down barriers between those of different backgrounds and faiths, we would love to hear from you at education@tonyblairfaithfoundation.org.

- Finally, the Foundation wants to identify the best resources and practices from across the world and ensure that these are made visible and accessible to all. Whether you are a teacher, an academic, a faith leader or parent, we would welcome your recommendations of high-quality materials that contribute to improving young people's religious literacy and understanding of the positive values of the great faiths.

The Tony Blair Faith Foundation has also joined forces with Yale University to launch the *Faith and Globalization Initiative*. This project academically explores religious faith as it impacts the modern world, with the hope of inspiring future educational research along the same lines. Tony Blair notes the following about this joint venture (Tony Blair Faith Foundation, 2008):

> Global interdependence is a reality. And faith is inextricably linked to that interdependence. As we have seen, faith can be a source of division and destruction. But faith can also be a source of reconciliation, not conflict.
>
> The Tony Blair Faith Foundation aims to promote the positive role of the world's faiths in the global realities of the twenty-first century, and to demonstrate the positive results that people of diverse faiths, working together, can accomplish.
>
> One key way in which the foundation hopes to accomplish these aims is through education. And so we are delighted to be partnering with Yale University, and with the Yale Divinity School and the Yale School of Management, to create the Faith and Globalization seminar.
>
> We intend for the Yale Faith and Globalization seminar to stimulate important academic research for anyone who is interested in learning about the world's diverse religions and their potential roles for the greater public good in the global economy. Faith can serve as a means for peace, progress, and prosperity for all of the peoples of the world.

In short, faith-based organizations provide a commendable and praiseworthy service to the world by helping those in need and encouraging tolerance of those who are different. Other organizations and groups do the same, but they do not always use faith as a major guiding principle.

Final Thoughts

For many people, faith got them to where they are today…and it will take them where they want to go tomorrow. Without their faith, they would find it more difficult to overcome obstacles as they strive to meet goals and become accomplished. Faith carries people through the bad times and propels them into the good…and this is sometimes only understood by those who believe.

Faith is a catalyst that drives people's thoughts and actions. Many people would not have achieved the success they did in life without faith. This success is unlimited and has no borders. It can be physical, mental, spiritual, or material; and it can include family, finance, politics, religion, or any other aspect of living that involves reaching a plateau or accomplishing a goal. This speaks mountains for the value of faith and the role that it plays in life.

Faith helps the decision-making process by providing guidance and direction; it heals physical and mental wounds through a belief that things will improve; and it changes perception of life's challenges to a more positive outlook. For some people, faith is important for getting through each and every day. For others, it is essential for attaining higher plateaus…and still other folks find faith to be the final frontier before entering the afterworld. In a world that is constantly evolving with new technology, *kneemail* might still be better than *email*.

Exercise your soul by running with your faith. Believe…and you will see!

References Cited

Albuquerque Buddhist Fellowship Group (2001). BUDDHIST FAITH AND INNER PEACE. Internet at http://buddhistfaith.tripod.com/newmexico/id16.html on July 21, 2008.

AMERICAN HERITAGE DICTIONARY (1982). 2nd college edition. Houghton, Mifflin: Boston, MA. Hard copy.

AMISH FORGIVENESS (2008). Internet at http://www.800padutch.com/amishforgiveness.shtml on January 30, 2009.

Bays, Patricia (1996). MEET THE FAMILY: WELCOME TO THE ANGLICAN CHURCH OF CANADA. ABC Publishing: Kitchener, Ontario, Canada. Hard copy.

BBC (2008, November 2). RELIGION & ETHICS – MORMONISM. Internet at http://www.bbc.co.uk/religion/religions/mormon/beliefs/other.shtml on November 2, 2008.

Bistrich, Andrea (2007, September). Discovering the common ground of world religions: Interview with Karen Armstrong. SHARE INTERNATIONAL. 26/7. 19–22. Internet at http://www.unaoc.org/repository/armstrong_interview.pdf on October 5, 2009.

COURAGE IN THE FACE OF NAZI PERIL (2008). Internet at http://www.watchtower.org/e/19980708/article_01.htm on December 28, 2008.

Curry, Erin (2003, September 12). THOUGH DRUGS & ALCOHOL HAD PLAGUED HIM, JOHNNY CASH WAS STEADIED BY HIS FAITH. Internet at http://jmm.aaa.net.au/articles/4802.htm on August 4, 2008.

D'Amico, John (2007, December). ASK AND YOU WILL RECEIVE: CREATING FAITH-BASED PROGRAMS FOR FORMER INMATES. Internet at http://findarticles.com/p/articles/mi_hb6399/is_6_69/ai_n29401712/pg_1?tag=artBody;coll on January 4, 2009.

Eckstrom, Kevin (2006, February 3). BONO, AFTER YEARS OF SKEPTICISM, FINDS A PARTNER IN RELIGION. Internet at http://www.atu2.com/news/article.src?ID=4225&Key=&Year=&Cat= on August 4, 2008.

FAITH-BASED GROUPS HELP EX-OFFENDERS (2003, August 7). Internet at http://alcoholism.about.com/cs/issues/a/blui030806.htm on August 6, 2008.

GENEVA SPIRITUAL APPEAL (2003). Internet at http://www.unhchr.ch/html/menu2/spirit.htm on February 5, 2009.

GOD VS. DOCTOR: 1 IN 2 SAY PRAYER SAVES THE DYING (2008, August 18). Internet at http://www.msnbc.msn.com/id/26272687 on August 29, 2009.

Interfaith Youth Core (2009). WHAT DO WE DO? Internet at http://www.ifyc.org/ on January 7, 2009.

International AIDS Society (2008, July 30). OPENING REMARKS OF THE FAITH-BASED ORGANIZATIONS MEETING. Internet at http://www.iasociety.org/Web/WebContent/File/Faith-Based%20Opening%20Remarks%2030-07-08.pdf on January 7, 2009.

JAINISM (n.d.). Internet at http://www.crystalinks.com/jainism.html on October 13, 2008.

Koehler, George E. (2006). THE UNITED METHODIST MEMBER'S HANDBOOK. Internet at http://www.umc.org/site/c.lwL4KnN1LtH/b.2295473/k.7034/Mission_and_Ministry.htm on August 11, 2008.

Kriegel, Mark (2009, January 16). FAITH DRIVING WARNER IN ANOTHER SUPER BOWL PURSUIT. Internet at http://msn.foxsports.com/nfl/story/9084852/Faith-driving-Warner-in-another-Super-Bowl-pursuit?MSNHPHMA on January 24, 2009.

Long, Jim (1998, March/April). GIVE ME PATIENCE…NOW. Internet at http://www.christianitytoday.com/cl/8c5/8c5010.html on July 9, 2008.

Lundy, S., and Roberts, L. (2007, February 5). FAITH BRINGS HOPE TO THE GRIEVING: RELIGIOUS SERVICES GO ON AMID THE RUINS. Internet at http://www.orlandosentinel.com/orl-mstormchurch0507feb05,0,7419279.story?page=1 on August 6, 2008.

Moss, Aron (2004, August 16). INNER PEACE. Internet at http://www.israelnationalnews.com/Articles/Article.aspx/4061 on July 29, 2008.

Oni, Adebola A. (2006). THE ASTOUNDING POWER OF FAITH. Internet at http://www.buzzle.com/editorials/6-20-2006-99829.asp on August, 3, 2008.

Papademetriou, George C. (2009). AN ORTHODOX REFLECTION ON TRUTH AND TOLERANCE. Internet at http://www.goarch.org/ourfaith/ourfaith8075 on January 31, 2009.

Peterson, Greg (2008, June 6). LUTHERAN MINISTER, BISHOP, ZEN BUDDHIST HEAD PRIEST TALK ABOUT CREATING INTERFAITH ENVIRONMENT PROJECTS. Internet at http://www.gather.com/viewArticle.jsp?articleId=281474977364041 on January 27, 2009.

Pringle, G. (2006, June 2). MY FAITH HELPS ME THROUGH HARD TIMES. Internet at http://findarticles.com/p/articles/mi_qn4158/is_20060602/ai_n16461162 on July 30, 2008.

REFORM TAOIST CONGREGATION (2007, December 30). Internet at http://www.reformtaoism.org/ on July 27, 2008.

RELIGIONS OF THE WORLD: SHINTO (2007). Internet at http://www.religioustolerance.org/shinto.htm on August 10, 2008.

RELIGIOUS AMERICANS: MY FAITH ISN'T THE ONLY WAY (2008, June 23). Internet at http://www.msnbc.msn.com/id/25334489 on July 9, 2008.

RELIGIOUSLY MOTIVATED VIOLENCE, MURDER, MASS MURDER, TERRORISM, AND GENOCIDE (2006). Internet at http://www.religioustolerance.org/relviol.htm on February 2, 2008.

Rizvi, Sayyid Muhammad (n.d.). AN INTRODUCTION TO ISLAM. Internet at http://www.al-islam.org/begin/intro/rizvi.html on July 17, 2008.

Russell, Maria T. (2007). PATIENCE. Internet at http://innerself.ca/Reflections/patience.htm on October 15, 2008.

Sears, D. (1998). COMPASSION FOR HUMANITY IN THE JEWISH TRADITION. Jason Aronson: Lanham, MD. Hard copy.

SHAMAN'S CREED (2008, October 25). Internet at http://www.shamanicnortheast.org on December 29, 2008.

SHARED BELIEF IN THE GOLDEN RULE (2006). Internet at http://www.religioustolerance.org/reciproc.htm on February 2, 2009.

Smith, Greg (2008, June 23). U.S. RELIGIOUS LANDSCAPE SURVEY REPORT II. Internet at http://pewforum.org/events/?EventID=190#fl on August 24, 2008.

St. Jude Children's Research Hospital. (2008). DANNY'S PROMISE. Internet at http://www.stjude.org/stjude/v/index.jsp?vgnextoid=576bfa2454e70110VgnVCM1000001e0215acRCRD&vgnextchannel=5af213c016118010VgnVCM1000000e2015acRCRD on October 13, 2008.

STUDY: RELIGIOUS FAITH IS BENEFICIAL FOR PATIENTS, AMERICAN DOCTORS BELIEVE (2007, April 22). Internet at http://www.vitabeat.com/study-religious-faith-is-beneficial-for-patients-american-doctors-believe/v/6071/ on October 15, 2008.

TEEN WHO LOST ARM TO ALLIGATOR: GOD WAS WITH ME (2008, June 25). Internet at http://www.msnbc.msn.com/id/25363093/ on July 4, 2009.

Tony Blair Faith Foundation (2008). MISSION STATEMENT. Internet at http://tonyblairfaithfoundation.org/about-us/mission-statement.html on January 13, 2009.

TRAGIC SHOOTING AT AN AMISH SCHOOL (2008). Internet at http://www.800padutch.com/amishshooting.shtml on January 30, 2009.

Turo-Shields, Dave (2007). FAITH AND DEPRESSION. Internet at http://www.selfgrowth.com/articles/Turo-Shields5.html on October 17, 2008.

UNDERSTANDING ISLAM AND MUSLIMS (1989). Internet at http://www.islamicity.com/mosque/uiatm/un_islam.htm on July 29, 2008.

Van Marsh, Alphonso (2007, December 23). U.S. TROOPS TURN TO FAITH AMID REALITIES OF WAR. Internet at http://www.cnn.com/2007/WORLD/meast/12/23/faith.base/index.html on November 10, 2009.

Warren, Lee (n.d). THE SACRED WRITINGS OF THE MAJOR WORLD RELIGIONS, EASTERN RELIGIONS. Internet at http://www.occult-advances.org/nc-rel-sacred-writings.shtml on October 1, 2009.

Willis, Andre C. (2008, November 17). FAITH-BASED POLITICS, THE OBAMA WAY. Internet at http://www.theroot.com/id/48879?GT1=38002 on November 20, 2008.

World Health Organization (2008). FAITH-BASED ORGANIZATIONS PLAY A MAJOR ROLE IN HIV/AIDS CARE AND TREATMENT IN SUB-SAHARAN AFRICA. Internet at http://www.who.int/mediacentre/news/notes/2007/np05/en/index.html on October 13, 2008.

Zaleski, Jeff, and Doto, Robert. (Spring 2007). SEVEN GREAT ACTS OF FAITH. PARABOLA. Internet at http://www.firstunitarianportland.org/sermons-publications/sermons-1/2007-sermon-file/finding-faith-in-a-sea-of-despair on August 9, 2008.

Zuckerman, Phil (2008). IS FAITH GOOD FOR US? Internet at http://www.secularhumanism.org/index.php?section=library&page=pzuckerman_26_5 on July 31, 2008.